Our World

Wood

By Kate Bedford

Aladdin/Watts
London • Sydney

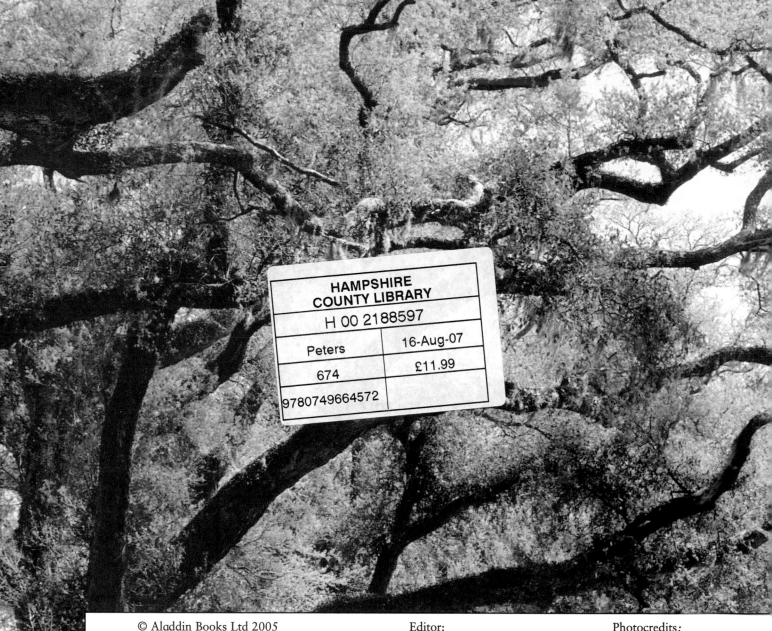

© Aladdin Books Ltd 2005

Designed and produced by
Aladdin Books Ltd
2/3 Fitzroy Mews
London W1T 6DF

First published in
Great Britain in 2005 by
Franklin Watts
96 Leonard Street
London EC2A 4XD

A catalogue record for this
book is available from the
British Library.

ISBN 0 7496 6257 3

Printed in Malaysia

Editor:
Harriet Brown

Designers:
Flick, Book Design and Graphics
Simon Morse

Picture Researcher:
Simon Morse
Brian Hunter Smart

Literacy consultant:
Jackie Holderness – former Senior
Lecturer in Primary Education,
Westminster Institute,
Oxford Brookes University

Illustrations:
Q2A Creative

CONTENTS

Notes to parents and teachers

This series has been developed for group use in the classroom as well as for children reading on their own. In particular, its differentiated text allows children of mixed abilities to enjoy reading about the same topic. The larger size text (A, below) offers apprentice readers a simplified text. This simplified text is used in the introduction to each chapter and in the picture captions. This font is part of the © Sassoon family of fonts recommended by the National Literacy Early Years Strategy document for maximum legibility. The smaller size text (B, below) offers a more challenging read for older or more able readers.

Wood from trees

The wood we use comes from two types of trees. These are called broad-leaved trees and conifers.

A

◀ **This oak tree is over 100 years old.**

Broad-leaved trees such as oak and maple have wide leaves. They grow in mild climates.

B

Questions, key words and glossary

Each spread ends with a question which parents and teachers can use to discuss and develop further ideas and concepts. Further questions are provided in a quiz on page 30. A reduced version of pages 30 and 31 is shown below. The illustrated 'Key words' section is provided as a revision tool, particularly for apprentice readers, in order to help with spelling, writing and guided reading as part of the literacy hour. The glossary is for more able or older readers. In addition to the glossary's role as a reference aid, it is also designed to reinforce new vocabulary and provide a tool for further discussion and revision. When glossary terms first appear in the text they are highlighted in bold.

 See how much you know!

What is charcoal made from?

Which insect makes its paper nest from wood?

Why does a tree have bark?

Why are fences sometimes put up around tree saplings?

What happens to the soil when rainforests are cut down?

How is paper made?

What happens to a tree when it dies?

How can you help to save trees?

Key words

Branch

A

Bark   Conifer   Forest
Knot   Log   Paper
Plank   Recycle   Trunk

Tree

Glossary

Fungi - Mushrooms, toadstools and moulds which feed on dead or living plants or animals.
Habitat - The place in which a plant or animal lives, such as a pond, wood or seashore.
Mosquito - An insect which feeds by sucking blood from humans or animals.
Nutrients - Simple parts of food that nourish plants and animals.
Pollution - Gases, chemicals or rubbish that damages the environment.
Rainforest - A forest that grows in places which are very hot and where it rains heavily almost every day.

B

Sustainable materials - Materials such as wood or wheat which can be grown again and again, and will not run out.
Sandpaper - Paper that is covered with sand on one side.

What is wood?

Wood is an amazing natural material. It is used every day all over the world. Wood is used to make many things. It was even used to make this book you are reading!

Branches

Trunk

Birch   Pine

◀ **Wood is found under the bark of trees.**

Wood comes from inside the trunks and branches of trees. The outside of a tree is covered with bark, which is like the tree's skin. The bark protects the wood on the inside from being attacked by insects, **fungi** and animals. Each kind of tree has its own special bark pattern, texture and colour.

▶ The dolls and the violin are made from wood.

Wood is strong, springy and warm to the touch. It can be cut, carved, shaped and coloured. Wood is used to build houses and to make furniture. Many musical instruments are made from wood.

Russian dolls   Violin

Early wooden sickle

Flint edge

Wood has been used by people for thousands of years.

People were using wood thousands of years ago before materials like metal were discovered. They used it to make tools, small boats like canoes and to build shelters. They burnt wood to keep warm, cook their food and to scare away wild animals at night.

Wooden plough

 What things have you used today that are made from wood?

7

Wood from trees

The wood we use comes from two types of trees. One type are called broad-leaved trees and the other type are called conifers. Broad-leaved trees grow slowly and have hard wood. Conifers grow much faster and their wood is usually softer.

◀ This oak tree is over 100 years old.

Broad-leaved trees such as oak and maple have wide leaves. Most broad-leaved trees are deciduous, which means they lose their leaves in the autumn. Broad-leaved trees usually grow in mild climates, but some grow in tropical rainforests. Timber from broad-leaved trees is known as hardwood.

 Most of our wood comes from conifers.

Conifer trees have needle-like leaves and grow well in cold conditions. They are grown in large forests called plantations. Plantations are like tree farms. The timber from conifer trees is called softwood.

Wood from conifers is used to build houses.

Fast growing softwood trees like Scots pine are used to make telegraph poles and the frames for some houses. Timber from slow growing hardwoods, such as oak, is used for making furniture.

 Can you name any trees that lose their leaves in the autumn?

Wood close up

Each year a tree grows a new layer of wood. The rings inside a tree trunk show each year's new growth. If you count the rings you can find out how old the tree is. This tree (right) is probably older than you.

Softwood

Knot

Grain

Hardwood

◀ **Knots show where a branch grew out from the tree trunk.**

The fibres make a pattern of lines called the grain. If the lines are close together, the wood is a hardwood. Broad-leaved trees have hardwood which is close-grained. If the lines of the grain are wider apart, the wood is open-grained or softwood. Conifers produce softwood.

Some wood is very strong.

Trees and other plants make a substance called cellulose. Cellulose forms into strands which matt together and make up the walls of tiny cells inside the tree. The cellulose is very important as it makes wood strong.

This board game is made from different colour woods.

Each type of tree has different coloured wood. Pine trees have a pale wood and walnut has a dark brown wood. A mixture of different colours of wood is sometimes used to decorate furniture.

 Can you find the grain pattern on a wooden object?

From seed to timber

Most of the wood we use is specially grown in large forests. These forests are carefully planned to help the trees grow well. The kind of trees planted are the ones that will grow best in the forest's soil and weather.

◀ **These baby trees are growing in a tree nursery.**

Conifer tree seeds are collected from pine cones in the autumn. Before they are planted, the hard seed coats are rubbed with **sandpaper** to help them grow quickly. The seeds are planted in paper containers and kept in a nursery to protect them from mice, birds and frost. Young trees are called saplings. They stay in the nursery for three years.

Trees are often planted by hand.

Before saplings are planted out, the soil is prepared with a digger or plough. The trees are planted close together to help protect them from the wind. Sometimes a fence is put up to stop deer or rabbits from nibbling the saplings.

When trees have grown big enough, they are cut down.

Conifers are cut down when they are 50-70 years old. Broad-leaved trees are left until they are 100-150 years old. Some trees are cut down by a woodcutter, or lumberjack, using a chain saw. Others are cut down with a harvester machine.

 How high must a fence be to stop deer nibbling saplings?

Moving and cutting

After the trees are cut down they are taken away. Most logs are carried out of the forest on special lorries or trains. They are taken to a sawmill. At the sawmill, huge saws can quickly cut up large tree trunks.

◀ **Animals can be used to pull logs out of the forest.**

In some forests, big machines cannot be used. In these places animals, such as horses or elephants, are used to transport logs out of the forest. The animals can easily move between growing trees and do not harm the environment.

▶ A saw cuts the tree into planks.

At the sawmill the bark is trimmed off and the logs are cut into planks. Logs can be cut in different ways to give different grain patterns. Hardwoods can be cut into thin slices called veneers. Veneers are used to decorate objects.

These planks are drying.

The cut planks cannot be used straight away because they still contain a lot of sap. Sap is the liquid or juice inside the wood. Freshly cut wood is called 'green' timber and needs to be dried out so that it will not twist, bend, crack or shrink when it's used. Drying the wood is called seasoning.

In which countries might you see elephants pulling logs?

Woodwork

Wood is a very useful material and is used to make many things. It is easy to cut into different shapes. It can be smoothed and polished. Objects made from wood can last for hundreds of years if they are looked after.

◀ **A carpenter's tools help to shape the wood.**

A person who makes things with wood is called a carpenter. Carpenters use tools to make wood into many different things such as furniture, toys and houses. The carpenter uses special tools such as saws, drills and chisels to cut and shape wood. They smooth wood by using sandpaper.

◄ Baskets are made from long, thin pieces of wood.

Thin branches of wood such as willow and hazel can bend easily. They are used to weave baskets of all shapes and sizes. Before weaving, the thin branches are soaked in water to help them bend easily and take shape.

These boats are made from tree trunks.

Wood can float and is often used to make boats. People who live by rivers in **rainforests** make boats from whole tree trunks. They cut down a straight tree and remove the bark. Then they hollow out the tree trunk by carefully burning the wood a little at a time. Finally they carve it out with tools. These boats are called dug-out canoes.

 How many things in your bedroom are made from wood?

Wood for fuel

Many people all over the world use wood for burning. Wood is a source of energy. When it burns, it gives out heat and light. People collect wood and use it to cook their food and to keep warm.

◀ **This meal is being cooked on a wood fire.**

In some places people cook food in a pot balanced over the flames of an open fire. As wood burns, it gives off smoke and grows smaller until all that is left is a grey ash. Wood smoke can pollute the air. To reduce this **pollution**, it is better to burn dry hardwood as it gives off less smoke than 'green' wood.

▶ This wood is being changed into charcoal.

Charcoal is made from wood that has been partly burnt. It is made by burning wood very slowly. After a few days, the wood turns into black charcoal. Charcoal can be used to draw with and is used as fuel. People use charcoal to cook on barbecues.

This car uses a fuel that can be made from wood.

Wood can be used to make a fuel called wood alcohol, or methanol. Methanol fuel is used to run cars and is even used by the racing cars in the Indianapolis 500 speedway races. Cars that use methanol fuel are cleaner and produce less pollution.

 Why do houses with coal fires need chimneys?

Wood for medicine and food

Many of the foods and medicines we use come from rainforest trees and plants. It is important to look after our rainforests, because many more useful medicines could be found in them in the future.

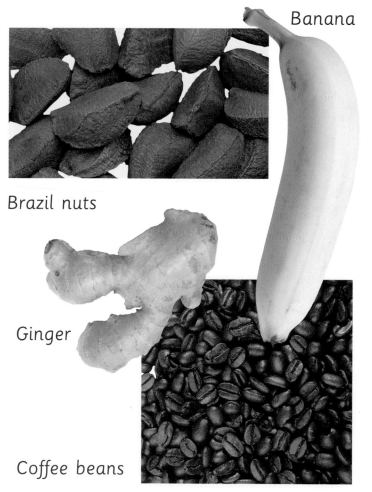

Brazil nuts

Ginger

Coffee beans

Banana

◀ **All these things come from rainforests.**

Lots of the foods that we eat come from rainforest trees and plants. Plants like pineapple, coffee and banana first grew wild in rainforests and are now grown on large plantations. Brazil nuts are still collected from trees growing in the rainforest.

◄ **The bark from this rainforest tree has saved many lives.**

The bark of the cinchona tree contains the chemical quinine. Quinine is used to treat the disease malaria which is passed to humans by **mosquitoes**. Quinine is also used as an antiseptic, an insect repellent and a sun cream.

When rainforest trees are cut down the soil washes away.

Rainforests grow on shallow soil which is low in **nutrients** (goodness). Trees can only grow on this poor soil if it is made fertile by fallen leaves and dead animals being recycled into the soil. When a rainforest is cut down, the nutrients in the soil wear out and are not replaced. Without trees, the soil dries up and is washed away, leaving the land like a desert.

 What foods do you eat that come from rainforest plants?

Paper-making

Most of the conifer trees grown in plantations (tree farms) are used to make paper. Paper is made by squashing, mixing and drying small wood fibres. You can see the tiny fibres when you tear a piece of paper.

◀ **Wood chips are made into paper at a paper mill.**

Paper is made at a factory called a paper mill. At the paper mill, logs are cut up into small wood chips. They are then squashed and pulped in machines until the wood is soft and spongy. The pulp is then mixed with chemicals to make a wet sludge.

▶ Paper is made into huge rolls.

The wood fibres in the sludge are squashed together and pressed into thin sheets of paper. Rollers squeeze out the water and the paper is dried and wound onto huge reels ready for use.

Toilet tissue

Writing paper

Cereal box

There are many different kinds of paper.

Wood pulp is made into many different kinds of paper, card and cardboard. Paper can be coloured with dye and made into different textures. Some paper is soft and can easily tear. It is used to make tissues and napkins. Cardboard is strong, thick and stiff and is made into boxes.

 What types of paper do you use at home and at school?

Wood for animals

Many animals use wood. Some use it as a building material to make their homes. Other animals eat wood. Animals like woodworm sometimes eat the wood we use inside our homes and leave it full of holes. They can harm whole houses.

◀ **Termites can also damage wooden houses.**

Most animals can't eat wood because it contains tough cellulose. Termites can eat wood because they have tiny creatures inside their gut which digest the cellulose for them. Termites live in the ground and dig tunnels into trees or wooden buildings. In some countries they are a problem because they damage wooden buildings.

This wasps' nest is made from wood fibres.

Wasps use wood to make their delicate paper nests. They scrape wood from wooden sheds or fence posts and chew it into a pulp. Then they shape the pulp into a nest. When the pulp dries out it hardens into paper.

Beavers use wood to build their homes.

Beavers cut down trees and use them to dam up streams and create a new lake. They use the trees to build a safe home, called a lodge, in the middle of the lake. They store branches under water and then eat them in the winter.

 How does a beaver's home protect it from its enemies?

Wood for life

Trees are very important for all the life on Earth. They help control the world's weather and clean the air we breathe. They provide homes and food to many different animals. We need trees for life.

◀ **These rainforest trees give us oxygen.**

Trees and plants remove carbon dioxide gas from the Earth's atmosphere. They use it to make their food and release oxygen back into the air. Rainforests recycle huge amounts of air. Many rainforests are being cut down and may disappear. We must preserve them as they are so important for cleaning the air.

◀ This fungus is growing on a tree.

When a tree dies a fungus may use it for food. Fungi feed and grow on the dead wood. They make the wood slowly rot away and help to recycle the wood's nutrients back into the soil. The nutrients are then re-used by other plants.

Many insects feed on rotting wood.

Rotting wood provides food and shelter to many animals. Some beetle larvae burrow into the wood as they feed. Woodlice feed on the larvae. Woodpeckers feed on the woodlice and other wood-eating insects.

Some beetles and beetle larvae feed on wood.

 What would happen if there were no trees?

Wood for the future

Wood is a valuable material that is used every day all over the world. Trees give food and shelter to many animals and clean the air we breathe. It is important to look after trees. We can do this by caring for forests and by recycling paper.

◀ **Everyone must care for our world's forests.**

Wood that comes from a well-managed forest is sometimes labelled so that we know the forest is **sustainable**. This means that when trees are harvested more trees are planted in their place. If we look after trees and replace the ones we cut down we will never run out of wood.

◀ **Recycling one tonne of paper saves 17 trees.**

Millions of trees are cut down each year to provide the raw material for making paper. Logging destroys **habitats** that are full of plants and animals. By recycling our waste paper, we can help to protect natural habitats and save trees. We can all help to save trees by recycling our waste paper and by buying products made from recycled paper.

This symbol tells you if something can be recycled. ▶

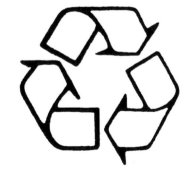

 What would happen if no-one recycled paper and card?

See how much you know!

What is charcoal made from?

Which insect makes its paper nest from wood?

Why does a tree have bark?

Why are fences sometimes put up around tree saplings?

What happens to the soil when rainforests are cut down?

How is paper made?

What happens to a tree when it dies?

How can you help to save trees?

Key words

Branch

Bark **Conifer** **Forest**

Knot **Log** **Paper**

Plank **Recycle** **Trunk**

Tree

Glossary

Fungi – Mushrooms, toadstools and moulds which feed on dead or living plants or animals.

Habitat – The place in which a plant or animal lives, such as a pond, wood or seashore.

Mosquito – An insect which feeds by sucking blood from humans or animals.

Nutrients – Simple parts of food that nourish plants and animals.

Pollution – Gases, chemicals or rubbish that damage the environment.

Rainforest – A forest that grows in places which are very hot and where it rains heavily almost every day.

Sandpaper – Paper that is covered with sand on one side. It used to smooth wood.

Sustainable materials – Materials such as wood or wheat which can be grown again and again, and will not run out.

Index